Weeping in the Promised Land

Weeping in the Promised Land

Poems by

Jennifer Lagier

© 2023 Jennifer Lagier. All rights reserved.
This material may not be reproduced in any form, published,
reprinted, recorded, performed, broadcast,
rewritten or redistributed without
the explicit permission of Jennifer Lagier.
All such actions are strictly prohibited by law.

Author and cover photos by Jennifer Lagier
Cover design by Shay Culligan

ISBN: 978-1-63980-402-3

Kelsay Books
502 South 1040 East, A-119
American Fork, Utah 84003
Kelsaybooks.com

For my poet mentors

Acknowledgments

Thank you to the following publications, where versions of these poems previously appeared:

Caesura: "A Painting No One Would Ever See"
Conceit Magazine: "Aurora Borealis," "When Women Were Birds"
Ethel: "Me & My Baby"
Five-Two Crime Poetry Blogspot: "Nothing is Normal Here," "Roe v. Wade Falls"
The Flying Dodo: "Ghosts of Christmases Past"
Harbinger Asylum: "Doors Don't Open," "Friends of the NRA"
Moss Piglet: "Your Friends"
Nerve Cowboy: "Scotch and Water"
Paterson Literary Review: "A Love Letter to My Father," "I Remember Him"
Poetrymagazine.com Anthology: "Full Moon"
Ravensperch: "What I Treasure"
The Rockford Review: "Old Ladies," "Sunshine"
San Francisco Peace and Hope, Honoring Ukraine: A Tribute: "Sunflowers," "Messenger," "Ukranian Nocturne"
Silver Birch Press: "Dialogues with the Dead," "Seduction," "How to Squander a Sunny Day"
Song of the San Joaquin: "Blackbirds"
Syndic Literary Review: "Language I Knew in Another Life," "Weeping in the Promised Land," "Uvalde Is Family to Me"
Winedrunk Sidewalk: "Crazy"

Contents

Young	15
Someplace Else	16
Language I Knew in Another Life	18
Unspoken	19
I Remember Him	20
Pseudo Son	21
Scotch and Water	22
Pastoral Counseling	23
Assimilation	24
Doors Don't Open	25
Somewhere	26
Ghosts of Christmases Past	27
Dialogues With the Dead	28
A Love Letter to My Father	29
What I Treasure	31
Weeping in the Promised Land	32
Messenger	33
Ukrainian Nocturne	34
Sunflowers	35
Nothing is Normal Here	36
Uvalde Is Family to Me	37
Friends of the NRA	38
Thoughts and Prayers	39
Woman's Body Is the Terrain on Which Patriarchy Is Erected	40
Roe v. Wade Falls	41
Aurora Borealis	42
Falling Stars	43
Guiding Light	44
Me & My Baby	45
Into the Woods	46
She Swims Laps in the Thunderstorm	47
A Painting Nobody Would Ever See	48

Eavesdropping in the Wild and Rooted Salon	49
Your Friends	50
Crazy	51
Procrastination	52
Old Ladies	53
Creaky Old Farts	54
Full Moon	55
The Crone's Secret	56
Clouds	57
A Few Small Nips	58
When Women Were Birds	59
Infinite Pacific	60
Blackbirds	61
Montegrey	62
Seduction	63
Anything Felt Possible	64
Night in Monterey	65
How to Squander a Sunny Day	66
Wild Turkeys	67
Soliloquy	68
A Hundred Songs	69
Sunshine	70

*Life isn't about waiting for the storm to pass . . .
It's about learning to dance in the rain.*
—Vivian Greene

Young

In every grammar school photo,
I looked about to cry,
cold sores sprinkled around
chapped, downturned lips.

Uncles called me Jumpy,
the skinny, nervous kid
with a sensitive stomach,
frequent nose bleeds, scabby knees.

In dad's orchard, I bloomed,
imbued with magical powers.
Could find hidden jackrabbit nests,
feral cats, coax wild squirrels
from the sanctuary of burrows.
Fit in better with creatures than people.

Someplace Else

*How often I found where I should be going
only by setting out for somewhere else.*
—R. Buckminster Fuller

Queen of interrupted trajectory,
I slingshot through life.
Career choices excite, then sour—
teacher, librarian, community organizer.
Nothing fills inner hunger.
Job descriptions and titles don't fit.

I am the discontented explorer
forever exchanging geography:
Escalon, Manteca, Modesto, Turlock,
outgrown villages clustered along Highway 99
as it bisects orchards, strip-malls,
arid, over-built Central Valley.

My horizons spread, first to Seattle,
then the Makah Indian Reservation
at the tip of Cape Flattery.
Later, I migrate to Berkeley,
live in a basement apartment
just up the street from Chez Panisse,
within walking distance of Telegraph Avenue,
the Polka Dot man, lavender lady blowing bubbles.

Now I've relocated to Steinbeck country.
In my Monterey neighborhood,
quiet nights bring the sound of surf,
cries from a few mournful seagulls.
A block from the stage where
Janis Joplin once wailed and
Jimi Hendrix torched his guitar,

I restore an octogenarian house,
nurture pink roses, scarlet salvia,
find serenity, make the earth flower.

Language I Knew in Another Life

from a quote by Diane Porter

I dream of long-dead aunts and uncles
seated at my great-grandmother's Sunday table.
Their voices raise in musical celebration,
an animated soundtrack of Italian dialect
no longer part of my world.

In sleep, I mimic their rowdy chorus,
throat sore from strangled subtext,
unable to repeat words or recreate melodies,
soundlessly mouthing songs.

Perhaps it's cultural self-censorship,
a lifetime of stifled stories,
omerta demanded by family loyalty,
refusal to spill their secrets,
reveal ancient history that could bury us all.

Unspoken

> *I wrote down everything that was left unsaid.*
> —Beau Beausoleil

Wordlessly, I knead affection
into hearty artisan bread,
slice homemade pasta,
compose a spicy peach cobbler,
sear marinated swordfish,
assemble zucchini torta.

My husband knows how to interpret
lavish culinary productions.
After dinner, he expresses appreciation
with a kiss, clears the table,
carries dirty dishes to kitchen counter.

At night, we fit together like lips
protecting a secret,
proclaim infinite love
in intimate silence.

I Remember Him

I see a version of my dad's smile
on my sister's face,
have inherited his stubby fingers,
wide feet and hammer toes
which strain my Birkenstock sandals.

He taught me how to shoot a .22 rifle,
then a 20-gauge shotgun,
the trick to driving a stick shift,
double clutching his yellow Bronco,
which levers and pedals to push
on the John Deere tractor.

He made me a substitute
for the son he never had,
took me pheasant hunting,
clam digging,
fishing in high Sierra streams
and the Stanislaus River.

At our local coffee house,
I bullshit with his surviving cronies,
laugh as we remember his various pranks,
can almost see him holding court at his favorite table.
He'd defy warnings from mom and doctor,
gobble forbidden maple bars,
knock back scalding black coffee with gusto.

Pseudo Son

Fathering only daughters,
dad did his best to transform me
into the son he would never have,
gifting me with cowboy boots, ten-gallon hat,
toy holster, revolvers.

As a teen, he taught me how to shoot a .22,
bought me fishing pole and tackle.
During summer, he depended on me
to drive his Caterpillar D-12,
ridge the orchard to prepare for flood irrigation.

Together, we climbed granite mountainsides,
fished high Sierra trout streams,
cooled off in Alpine lakes.
At night in primitive, pine canopied campsites,
we grilled our silver catch over crackling fire.

Scotch and Water

In a Quonset hut officers' club
at the Cape Flattery SAC airbase,
my husband would order
a scotch and water for me to nurse
throughout the night
as he got louder, more aggressive,
until falling-down drunk.

Young airmen who
observed my unhappiness,
galloped to the rescue.
Prince Charming wannabes
led me onto the dance floor,
tried every line in the book,
to get into my pants.

On my 20th birthday,
one brought me cake,
flowers, ordered champagne,
held my hand under the table,
offered to pick up the tab
for divorce, help me
make a fresh start.

Guilt-ridden, I turned him down,
assisted my sodden mate to our car
where he pissed himself,
puked all over the upholstery.
I drove us back to the Coast Guard station,
a single-wide trailer perched at cliff's edge,
the fragile cocoon we called home.

Pastoral Counseling

"Puberty begins under your arms,"
the parish priest earnestly explains
during our mandatory counseling session.
He instructs us on sex,
tells us laws of gravity must be observed
during marital embrace.

We're told to reject sinful birth control,
reproduce as often as God demands,
revere the sacraments, attend Sunday mass.
"It's the woman's role to model Mary,
pray, sacrifice, obey," he admonishes,
"Give your husband
unconditional love and respect."

I glare at this man in a dress,
Catholic cult-leader who probably prefers
his altar boys pre-pubescent,
vow to break as many archaic rules
as often as possible.
After an hour of misogynistic bullshit,
resolve to erase medieval dogma with tequila,
never set foot in Father O'Dollar's
grifter cathedral again.

Assimilation

My great-grandmother told stories about
fire that devoured their home in Piatta,
accidental deaths of siblings, bambinos.
She was silent on the subject of immigration
from Italy to Ellis Island, a sea voyage in steerage,
passing through cattle chute check points.

Retracing her steps, I am overwhelmed,
weep while passing sepia photos
of ragged families just like mine,
relatives rechristened with American names
as they entered this portal.

Each generation, our culture is watered down further,
tribe broken apart into nuclear groupings.
No more Sunday dinners eating ravioli, polenta,
learning our history from tales by the elders.

We reunite when surviving cousins
gather at weddings or funerals,
update our genealogical database
with who's deceased, new additions, addresses.
Every time, we vow to stay in touch,
maintain connections using telephone, email.

Doors Don't Open

The glass ceiling will go away when women help other women break through that ceiling.
—Indra Nooyi

Job interview questions during the 70's included:
"Are you on birth control?"
"Do you plan to get pregnant?"
"Will your husband mind if you work evenings and weekends?"

Women managers were the exception,
often mimed sexist male supervisors,
perpetuated arrogant misogyny
as a means of survival.

For years, I dreamed of earning a degree
to advance my academic career.
Became a dean to improve working conditions,
campus support for at-risk students.

Instead, I was the administrator
in charge on Saturdays, nights,
dealt with tach squad, FBI,
gang banger task force.

Drive-by shootings on campus
during my watch
left me with PTSD,
killed my soul, motivation.

Somewhere

He swears he's been two years sober
as she watches him sweat, puke, convulse
on emergency room gurney.
Nurses administer haldol, ativan, verced
which do nothing to ease
his violent withdrawals.
He thrashes, cries out,
begs someone to kill him.
At the moment, she is
more than willing to comply,
if provided a weapon.

Somewhere, happy couples
sip champagne,
organize exotic trips,
plan for their future.
This blueprint will
never be theirs.
"One day at a time,"
she reminds herself.
The doctor injects an antidote.
Her husband escapes into coma.

Ghosts of Christmases Past

I remember Christmas Eves spent in emergency rooms
after loved ones overdosed, suffered panic attacks,
convulsed and hallucinated from alcoholic withdrawals.

Holiday carols bring flashbacks of Christmas Day burns,
cuts and bruises, carving knife malfunctions
that resulted in stitches or severed pieces of fingers.

Each year resurrects ghosts: resentment, chest pains,
shingles, pneumonia.

All I want from Santa is an uneventful Noel
without blood or drama.

Dialogues With the Dead

She sits in memory care garden,
soaks up sunshine, lists her dead,
tries to remember their faces,
still waiting to hear voices silent for decades.

She asks if I knew her mother,
a skilled seamstress who died
in Germany twenty-five years
before I was born.

Random reminiscence floats to the surface,
temporarily claims her attention.
Cognition comes and goes,
a distracted trail that meanders.

I think of my father, obsessed
over elusive names which he scribbled
onto paper scraps, then hid in a shoebox,
clues we discovered once he was gone.

How long, I wonder, before
my mental train jumps the track,
one more declining senior citizen,
lost and befuddled.

A Love Letter to My Father

from an Edwaard Liang quote

Like all Lewis men before him,
he loved hunting, fishing,
dogs and his children.
Each morning, he roused us from bed,
singing at the top of his voice,
Every sleeper waken. The sun is in the sky.
Wake up! Wake up! And hear the cuckoo's cry.

He named me after actress Jennifer Jones,
did his best to turn me into the son
he'd never have, taught me farming,
how to drive the Caterpillar tractor,
a stick shift Mack truck,
bought me a 20-gauge shotgun.

When I was a skinny, self-conscious teen,
he took me to the high Sierras,
helped me scale rocky canyon walls,
slide Pautzke Balls of Fire onto a barbed lure,
cast my line into deep pools,
deftly hook rainbow trout.

As a married woman, I lived
on one of his almond ranches,
flood irrigated twenty acres of orchard,
assisted with autumn harvest,
hauled carts of nuts to the huller.

Later, as disabilities robbed him of mobility,
tethered to oxygen tank and walker,
he held court at the local coffee house,
bought me maple bars, black coffee,
joked with other aging, retired farmers.

On the drive home, he warbled,
The rings around her eyeballs were red instead of blue . . .
Congestive heart failure, spinal stenosis,
couldn't extinguish his unique sense of humor.

What I Treasure

I had no idea what would become precious.
—Megan Wilcher

Memories of my great-grandmother's Christmas gift:
Torrone almond nougat with a silver half dollar.

As a teen, trendy gauntness, pierced ears,
praise written on assignments by favorite teachers.

In my twenties, a return to California and college after
three years living in a trailer house on the Makah Reservation.

The divorce I fought to obtain the year I turned thirty.

Relocation from Central Valley to Monterey Peninsula
where I met my tribe—poets congregating in Café Portofino.

Earning a Ph.D. in my mid-fifties.

Marriage to my soul mate in Big Sur overlooking ocean
on cold, clear afternoon on the first of November.

Goddess friends who are always there with hot herbal tea,
hugs and sympathy when I most need them.

A library of poetry, garden overflowing with jonquils,
this day filled with hope, sunshine, birdsong.

Weeping in the Promised Land

inspired by a John Fogerty song

As America tears itself in two,
I find myself terrified,
too dispirited to mingle
despite pandemic's easing.
An ever-present urge to weep
shadows my every move,
infuses each day with growing depression.

Headlines inflame.
Sanity, empathy, kindness ebb.
We've reverted to cavemen,
nourish ourselves on soundbites of hatred.
Power is poison.
Racism rises.
Brutality rules.
Integrity branded a devil.

Profiled, scapegoated,
pulled over with little cause,
their homes invaded,
knees on necks,
bullets in flesh,
people cry, "I can't breathe,"
demand impartial justice.

From shore to shore,
those tasked to protect
turn a blind eye,
choose cruelty, murder.
Resentments fester.
Blood and tears flow.
Our silence equals complicity.

Messenger

I have come to understand
that we are all messengers to one another
　　　　　　—Beau Beausoleil

A woman stands in the war zone,
hands seeds to a soldier, tells him,
Take these and put them in your pocket,
so sunflowers will grow
when you all die here.

Golden petals crown lanky stalks,
sprout from ditch banks,
between tin-roof shacks,
along country roadsides.

Tenacious sun seekers
thrive despite inhospitable soil
Tokens of hope
lift heavy heads toward light,
above barbed wire boundaries.

Passing jays drop sunflower seeds
among lupine, poppies, alyssum—
a promise that winter's passage
will blossom healing and peace.

Ukrainian Nocturne

As if to music, as if to peace.
—Eavan Boland

Each night, nameless men
switch street signs
to misdirect enemy soldiers.
An old woman sets her cat carrier
near a pile of rubble,
scavenges smoldering ruins
for surviving mementos.

In a crowded subway station,
underneath burning wreckage,
a little girl dreams of peace,
snuggles doggie and doll,
imagines blue summer sky,
running barefoot through tranquil field,
rows of golden sunflowers.

Sunflowers

From distant first world safety,
we shudder at worsening headlines,
witness family homes, maternity hospital,
theater clearly marked as a refuge
harboring women and children
transformed to rubble.

While we paint fire hydrants blue and yellow,
fly the Ukrainian flag over Monterey city hall,
from boat masts in protected marina,
defiant war zone survivors take back their cities,
deliver water and food, rescue the fallen,
replace street signs with taunts targeting Putin.

Around the planet,
sunflowers rise in solidarity,
push golden faces toward light,
towering blooms that symbolize
resistance, persistence, a desire for peace.

Nothing is Normal Here

*Over the next two-and-a-half traumatic weeks,
the Uvalde community will say goodbye to the
19 children and two teachers killed in a mass shooting.*
                              —Huffington Post

In grammar school,
we practiced duck and cover,
huddled under clunky desks,
laughable attempts to survive
being vaporized by nuclear missiles.
Might as well kiss our asses goodbye,
bigger kids used to joke.
Now ten-year-olds wear backpacks
that double as bullet proof vests,
rehearse active shooter drills.

One young girl describes smearing
her wounded body with a murdered friend's blood,
plays dead to avoid additional bullets,
watches classmates, teachers slaughtered
during the hour they were trapped in a room
with a teen wielding an AR-15
while police waited outside.

Politicians who receive
the largest NRA contributions
deliver limp platitudes,
empty hopes, stale prayers.

Nothing changes.
More lives are lost.

Uvalde Is Family to Me

It's personal.
Before Columbine, Sandy Hook, Stoneman Douglas,
a teen gunman with a grudge against immigrants
entered Cleveland Elementary School in Stockton,
slaughtered five Vietnamese students.
These were my kids, shy readers who hung out
in our small storefront library.

Angry males with automatic rifles
vent rage by mowing down youngsters.
Politicians funded by NRA blood money
worship a misconstrued second amendment,
mumble about the inevitability of violence,
refuse to consider common sense gun control.
In response, journalists debate publishing photos
of what military-grade firearms
can do to a body.

The Uvalde carnage wounds us all,
tears apart community,
leaves families traumatized
as they mourn catastrophic loss,
bury their loved ones.
We the People grieve,
reject platitudes, demand action,
implore our representatives
to protect children, not weapons.

Friends of the NRA

Not school children or teachers
slaughtered in a rain of bullets
by disgruntled white men.

Not women assassinated
during yet another
misogynistic, psychotic break.

Not those with brown skin
gunned down without consequences
by gung-ho, militaristic police.

Not the victims
of domestic terrorism
at Planned Parenthood clinics.

Not survivors of Columbine,
Sandy Hook, Parkland,
Las Vegas, San Bernardino.

Friends include bought off politicians,
well-paid lobbyists, Russian money launderers,
conspiracy theorists, right-wing militia.

Miscreants roll out the red carpet,
invite Ares, Mammon and their cruel associates
to the biggest gun show in town.

Thoughts and Prayers

> *'Really angry' gunman who killed 3 at Gilroy Garlic Festival cut fence, shot randomly for less than a minute.*
> —USA Today

While I attend a Monterey poetry reading where
two Latino poets promote love and unity,
one more furious white man cuts through a fence,
with his automatic rifle, shoots down
fifteen festival attendees, killing three,
including a six-year-old boy,
thirteen-year-old girl.

When will we, as a nation,
discontinue spewing useless aphorisms,
no longer facilitate poison
seeping into hearts and minds,
bind wounds, staunch hatred,
reject division, halt wanton bleeding?

When do we quit mouthing platitudes,
lance festering resentments,
drain away sickness, cauterize anger,
make America safe and sane again,
put rational adults
in charge of our healing?

Please, no more thoughts and prayers.
We need moral leadership, action.

Woman's Body Is the Terrain on Which Patriarchy Is Erected

from a quote by Adrienne Rich

My great grandmother pushed forth babies,
hauled wood like a pack horse,
tended the garden, scrubbed floors,
worked in the fields.

My grandmother survived
her abusive, alcoholic husband,
accepted charity when he died of cirrhosis
leaving her to raise four little girls.

In high school during WWII, mom and my aunts
were cheated of teenage dances and dates,
got cannery jobs, married early,
juggled home, extended family, children.

The men in their lives siphoned off
youth, energy, possibilities,
left them filled with resentment,
angry about sabotaged opportunities.

I learn from matriarchal example,
reject fairytales, subvert patriarchy,
embrace independence,
carve my own unique trail.

Roe v. Wade Falls

In June, the Supreme Court decimated nearly 50 years of established abortion law and handed abortion rights over to the states, unleashing legal chaos. Thanks to "trigger" laws springing into effect, Civil War era bans being resurrected and an overall legal uncertainty that combined with high criminal penalties, many clinics ceased abortion services or closed entirely.

—The Hill

An Antonin Scalia handmaid,
joined by spiteful male Supremes,
two accused of sexual misconduct,
gleefully usurp a woman's right
to control her own body.
Misogyny informs their decision,
a bully's need to press jackboots
upon the neck of sisters, daughters and mothers.

Outraged Americans spill into the streets,
protest draconian overturn of fifty-year-old law.
One justice vows to ban contraception,
roll back LGBTQ rights, recriminalize miscegenation,
resegregate schools, encourage persecution, repression.

Who knew in my lifetime
the dark ages would stage a comeback,
democracy corrupted, deformed
into a cruel, intolerant Gilead theocracy
funded by Federalists and the NRA,
a nightmare more horrific than fiction?

Aurora Borealis

for my cousin's daughter

How rapidly after the girl
fell into bottomless Alaskan crevasse,
did she realize there would be no escape?

As she slid down blue abyss,
her desperate hands clawed icy walls
for unattainable purchase.

In those final moments, did angels sing
while her body plummeted
and severed soul ascended?

Native Americans say the dead
become northern lights,
dance across night sky.

Ancestral spirit guides flare
above glacial crypt.

Falling Stars

Lime green asteroids speckle night sky.
Skeletal sycamore rakes bare fingers
across stippled horizon, writhing limbs
reflect against taut mirror
of cobalt blue pond.

This is how creativity descends,
startling flames of mysterious epiphany
that ignite, sear the soul.
Art sustains and transforms.

Guiding Light

Rising winds push ocean waves and charcoal fog
against headlands
guarded by a semi-circle of granite boulders.
Beneath red-turreted roof, a brilliant Fresnel lens
pours guiding light toward approaching ships,
offers safe passage for those adrift
seeking protective harbor.

In his white cottage on exposed cliff edge,
the lighthouse keeper watches roiling sea,
sips an enamel mug filled with bitter black coffee.
It's a lonely, but contemplative life,
serving as surrogate guardian angel
for sailors battling storms,
treacherous shores,
menacing walls of virulent water.

During these times of division,
dramatic climate change,
we crave deliverance
to sheltered destinations,
navigation assisted by benevolent beacon.

Me & My Baby

Sepia toddler with flyaway curls
wears checked gingham, bejeweled Mary Janes,
clutches her cloth dolly by one tubular arm.
Chin down, face askance, she evades camera lens.

Beyond this frame, her mother
exerts insistent influence,
flings sharp orders that penetrate,
leave permanent wounds.

Pain shadows the little girl's eyes.
She knows if she fidgets
or musses her clothes,
harsher reprimands will descend.

Stereotypical presentation is the point.
She is as powerless as her yarn-haired baby,
a near-infant being groomed to attract a mate,
care for a flesh and blood child.

Into the Woods

Seductive ribbon curves through feathery grove,
invites restless hiker to pass
between tangled brambles,
ascend rutted hillside.

Underneath fallen tree trunks,
scolding squirrels burrow under oak duff,
small bunnies hide.
Inland wind ruffles green canopy,
agitates blue jays, spills sparrows
who chatter, litter leaf-decoupaged ground.

This is fertile territory
for a sequestered recluse
who escapes fifteen months of isolation,
craves an unexplored trail,
ridge top views of Monterey Bay,
discovery of fossilized shells
embedded in shale.

She Swims Laps in the Thunderstorm

for Nancy M. (1924–2020)

I remember her, tiny-boned, blonde,
spilling nervous energy.
She sits at the lunch counter,
desegregating a Detroit restaurant.
Moving to Monterey, she became an educator,
designed curriculum, insisted the school district
offer vocational programs.

As a leader in the Women's International
League of Peace and Freedom,
she traveled to China and Cuba,
organized the Clothesline Project,
participants creating and displaying shirts
commemorating victims of violence.

On Earth Day, she dressed as a waitress
from the New World Order Cafe,
passed out menus itemizing the cost of weapons,
suggested alternative expenditures of taxpayer dollars:
healthcare, childcare, education and housing.

Her paint-free, self-plumbed cottage
always had a spare bed, cold beer,
pool table, bubbling hot tub,
offered sanctuary for broken war vets,
traumatized women
in the midst of transition.

Short-haired, devilish blue eyes,
she marched, petitioned, picketed,
demanded honesty, accountability,
nagged senators and congressmen,
had their home numbers on speed dial,
held their feet to the fire.

A Painting Nobody Would Ever See

My brother-in-law is dead.
His misogynist portraits
of unhappy, distorted women
who got between him and the bottle
hang like trophies
on my ex-husband's walls.

Their alcoholic father was also
a moody artist who threw away his career.
During one drunken rampage,
he sabotaged a New York opening,
slashed and smashed paintings,
trashed the gallery,
insulted his patron.

These men dedicated their lives
in a relentless dive to the bottom.
They left behind wives, lovers, children,
boxes of unread poetry,
unseen canvases,
passed on a legacy
of anger, addiction.

Eavesdropping in the Wild and Rooted Salon

As COVID pandemic enters year three,
a quartet of masked geriatric women
shuffle into a Carmel beauty salon.
Hairdressers, swathed in protective gear,
tint, style, condition shaggy manes
that have devolved into snarls of varying colors.

One offers her clientele
a range of possible options:
short locks, long tresses,
curls, ringlets, bobs,
daring purple extensions.

Another shares a trash magazine article
that suggests we can sleep
with men, women, both,
remain in an isolated bubble
or explore our repressed passions,
stretch the old boundaries.

Beneath plastic dryers, terrycloth capes,
elderly women savor shared cackles,
volunteer irreverent commentary,
reach consensus—it all
sounds too exhausting.

Your Friends

Your cronies call each other goddesses,
dress in exotic gowns,
wear faux tiaras on birthdays,
are the subjects of curious gossip,
hang out at bohemian bars
in the wilds of Big Sur.

We have each other's back,
listen without judgement,
commiserate during breakups,
hookups, illness, infirmity,
financial hardship,
family deaths.

We exchange house keys,
security codes,
Internet passwords
Share names of physical therapists,
massage technicians,
female physicians.

As we age, vow to start
our own geriatric commune.
Can't imagine life
without this supportive sisterhood
of sympathetic soulmates,
irreverent friends.

Crazy

I notice as a woman in the pharmacy
check-out line unloads her basket:
home pregnancy test, bag of Doritos,
midnight blue eyeliner,
toy Jedi light saber.

She flaunts chipped ebony toenails,
wears faded Levi's.
Her torn Metallica tee shirt
clings by a thread,
has seen better days.

The cashier asks about my husband,
now two years into sober recovery.
She was concerned when he stopped
buying bottles of Crown Royal daily
on his way to and from work.

A drunk, homeless man hits me up
for a dollar as I walk to my car.
We're part of the unraveling social asylum,
look for whatever erases or numbs,
doing what we can to get by.

Procrastination

Chirping smoke alarms
join the refrigerator's
change filter message
in being ignored.
Printer ink cartridges have been
depleted for over two years.
A neglected jury summons
gathers dust on the counter.

Her insurance non-renewal notice
languishes among growing piles
of correspondence, overdue bills.
Deadlines for late IRS filings
have come and gone
with no further attention.

Manana is her mantra,
a naïve belief problems
will solve themselves
without intervention.
"I'll get around to it,"
she assures me.
We both know she won't.

Old Ladies

The dental hygienist is teary,
complains of an alcoholic husband,
in and out of rehab,
who always stops at a liquor store
to pick up a fifth on his way home.
He spends nights and evenings
in a drunken coma,
hallucinates and becomes abusive
when he wakes up.
She has filed for separation,
persuaded him to sign over to her
the deed to their house.
Now she wants him out
but can't quite bring herself
to pack his shit,
leave it on the sidewalk,
obtain a restraining order,
call the police,
change all the locks.

We commiserate—
I've survived the identical nightmare,
midnight trips to Emergency,
seizures and atrial fibrillation,
public embarrassment,
lies that spill from his mouth.
She and I are too old to tolerate
another hour of captive misery,
compare notes on escape strategies,
vow to protect each other's back
as we disentangle from dysfunction,
reconstruct better lives,
find healthy ways to move on.

Creaky Old Farts

> *. . . hips and knees creak on their hinges.*
> —Joan Colby in Bony Old Folks

I observe cousins limping down the aisle
during my aunt's funeral.
One shifts painfully beside me,
unable to genuflect or kneel during
two and a half hours of memorial mass.

Looking around the parish hall,
I calculate how many have endured or require
hip and/or knee replacements,
wonder if we could negotiate
an economical group rate,
fantasize the small fortune
a good orthopedist could net.

Defective DNA predisposes us to osteoarthritis,
crumbling spines, degenerating joints,
Swiss Italians who lack cartilage.
Complaining, we creak through life,
hampered by immobility,
grind bone upon bone.

Full Moon

Summer heat manifests mist.
Fog slings a translucent scrim
between celestial dome
and impressionistic pond.
Moonlight haloes willow trees,
reverberates across dappled water.

This is my monochrome dream:
empty gray streets, ashy horizon,
vague charcoal ruins.
I float above earth's somber curve.
Below, splayed rows of leafless orchard.
Overhead, grim sky, smudged infinity.

Perhaps restorative raindrops will fall?

The Crone's Secret

A wise woman evolves from once-nubile nyphette,
shelters in the heart of a forest,
communes with foxes, squirrels, racoons.

She is apple-faced, enfolded in pansy print fabric.
White egrets flap across her bandanna.
She wears a gown of wing-spread doves, viola blooms.

Mother, maiden, goddess, she wraps fern cloak
around withered arms, angular shoulders.
Camoflauged by fissured tree bark, she merges with pines.

Wizened enchantress whispers ancient secrets
born of fin, fur, feather, cartilage, bone,
inscribes incantations for bewitchment, fertility.

Seer, healer, midwife, she pirouettes around popping fire.
On nights the moon swells, hangs in inky firmament,
she invokes fecund mysteries, calls forth buried life.

Clouds

August sautés golden hilltops.
Summer fog shreds itself into vapor confetti.
Tattered clouds reveal shocking blue.
A lone hawk keens, spins overhead.

Rattlesnake grass crackles as invisible lizards
scurry across fissured adobe.
Relentless sun taunts drooping pines.

Cumulus cast ephemeral shadows.
We crave their darker cousins,
pray for elusive rainstorms.
Persistent drought lingers.

A Few Small Nips

inspired by Frida Kahlo's painting of the same title

Passion guides the blade in a man's hand as
he slashes his lover's nude body.
The dead woman's face is turned,
Hair matted with gore, eyes tightly closed.

A black shoe remains on one foot.
The other has vanished.
Red spatters soak white sheet,
his shirt, dull yellow floor.

"A few small nips" reads the banner
towed across the crime scene
by blackbird and dove.
Bloody fingerprints disfigure the picture frame,
break the fourth wall.

She is the passive victim of perfidious butchery,
robbed of dignity, reduced to cautionary tale.
Those familiar with betrayal
understand how cumulative infidelities
bleed heart and soul dry.

When Women Were Birds

Once upon a time, when women were birds,
there was the simple understanding that
to sing at dawn and to sing at dusk
was to heal the world through joy.
　　　　　　—Terry Tempest Williams

Once wise women ruled,
taught children, cherished elders,
supported their sisters.

Back then, we could fly
above flowering plum trees
and golden fiddleneck fields.

We warbled goddess proverbs,
cultivated field and garden,
trilled forest news.

Flocks of swallows ascending,
we skimmed summer spindrift,
autumn's kelp-littered strand.

We clutched whiplash pine limbs,
endured buffeting squalls,
rode out winter storms.

Beneath rainbows, we gathered
in sun-lit poppy meadows,
birdsong healing torn world.

Infinite Pacific

The Infinite Ocean hovers in the space between life and death, when spirits must let go of whatever ties them to the physical world.
—Edwaard Liang, choreographer of *The Infinite Ocean*, performed by the SF Ballet.

Gray ocean pulses ashore, deposits torn seaweed.
Mist cloaks intertwined harbor seals,
a floating clump of silver whiskers, rubbery fins.
Triangular sails slice blurry horizon.
Two surfers await muscular surge of incoming waves.

To the east, trawling fishermen
harvest squirming yellowtail,
yank flat halibut from continental shelf,
dump gasping catch onto slick decks.
Gulls circle overhead and complain.

After sunset, a jagged platinum smear
paints reflected light across rippling saltwater,
joins night sky with sleepy harbor.
Bright ribbon of luminescence reveals
rising moon's radiant trail.

Blackbirds

Glossy blackbirds
flap from power lines
into succulent garden where they
peck apart snail shells,
swallow squirming earthworms
without thought or conscience.

Hunch-backed Igors
invoke gloomy gravestones,
bead silver oak limbs,
squawk disapproval,
circle neighborhood rooflines,
cawing ebony storm clouds.

Raving vagabonds ravage
rain-battered tomatoes,
excavate acorns
wedged between shingles,
leave chalky editorial comments
splatted on skylights.

Montegrey

Chill wraiths ooze between
pine-pelted mountain tops.
Damp mist scarfs boat masts,
digs pointed claws into arthritic joints.
Pallid light reveals drizzle.
Old bodies ache.

As triple digit heat
desiccates Central Valley,
coastal fog rolls ashore,
bejewels drooping hydrangeas
with delicate droplets.
Backyard roses rehydrate,
thirst slaked by cooling miasma.

Elsewhere, climate-changed summer simmers.
Glaciers melt; forests burn.
Here, bleak greyness, drippy morning.
Curdled sky triggers pain, sucks away joy,
portends poisoned earth,
polluted air, undrinkable water.

We are our own worst enemy,
value profits greater than life.

Seduction

. . . lured by the river-goddess in her sinuous and fitful bed.
—Joan Colby

Aphrodite tosses, turns a turquoise shoulder.
Spindrift nightdress floats atop curling surf.

Harbor seals keen, wail atop dry boulders,
crying for mates.

Promiscuous wisteria unwinds tentacled runners,
hauls itself along pergola, dangles lavender blooms.

Engorged moon attracts nocturnal raccoons.
They gather for careless orgies upon shingled roofs.

In dark bedroom, a man whispers enticements.
His bewitched lover offers herself like a sacrament.

Easter Sunday approaches. Resurrection arrives.
Rituals paused by pandemic living resume.

Anything Felt Possible

from a quote by Katrina Vandenberg

Quiet cessation of whispery drizzle
offers dry reprieve within which to ramble.
I have no fixed destination,
defer to whatever higher power
guides my feet onto sidewalks, trails,
damp strand of beach
where I sort through detritus,
looking for treasure.

Incoming sea breezes froth cobalt ocean.
On shore, spring pulses, erupts in pink blossoms,
ignites beach grass with embers of volatile poppies.
Willows cast off catkins, unfold tender foliage.
Coast chaparral spills drab sparrows, small bunnies.
Revived life emerges from a year's hibernation.
I stand upon an adobe bluff, awash with gratitude,
scan clearing horizon.

Night in Monterey

The world has a blue mask,
I live in its caves.
Only my footprints
are visible.
—Jane Rades, *Deer*

Tawny mountain lions cloaked in twilight
emerge from oak lands, creep along Frog Pond,
prowl hillsides in search of deer
during star freckled darkness.

Ring-tailed raccoons haul themselves out of storm drains,
pilfer banana peels, stale bread, soggy popcorn.
They topple bird baths while washing paws,
conduct noisy orgies on rooftops.

After sunset, tuxedoed skunks slink from bushes,
snug underground burrows.
Possums teeter along back yard fence line.
Feral eyes glitter through skylights.

Inspired by full moon,
erotic orange blossom perfume,
a man enfolds his lover, presses
her pale softness against flannel sheets.

How to Squander a Sunny Day

Spend the afternoon. You can't take it with you.
—Annie Dillard

Sunlight steams away nighttime drizzle,
flings coins of golden poppies
among lavender lupine.
Honeybees flaunt stockings of yellow pollen.
Blue jays spear slugs and snails,
glean pests from awakening garden.

A poet ignores dirty laundry,
abandons vacuuming, mopping.
Surrounded by primroses,
she props feet against oak barrel,
squanders warm afternoon,
scribbles on notepad.

Self-indulgent indolence seduces
hibernating muse from her shelter,
jump-starts imagination held hostage
by months of pandemic winter.
Spring revives taciturn earth
with lyrical hyacinths, cheery daffodil stanzas.

Wild Turkeys

Feathery Ichabod Cranes on the lam
emerge onto city streets from oak savanna.
Lanky explorers mosey down sidewalks
into front yards where they decimate lavender vinca.

When spooked, they flap awkward wings,
crash land atop a neighbor's shingled roof,
peer over redwood fence
into empty golf course and fair grounds.

I watch turkey triumvirate
swivel reptilian heads, shake droopy wattles,
gobble impatiently at one another as they
debate the best escape to avoid dinner platter.

Soliloquy

You aren't the first to starve with a pen in your hand.
—Grisel Y. Acosta

During third year of pandemic isolation,
immunocompromised, masked,
I hunger for music, theater, crowded restaurants,
remain sequestered behind a moat
of fear, rising infections, co-morbidities.

The dogs have become accustomed
to my 24/7 presence, constant attention.
I clean closets, reorganize cupboards.
Over coffee, I read a friend's new book,
summon my sullen, uncooperative muse.

The garden has never looked better.
I dead-head, pull weeds,
sow foxglove and lobelia seeds.
I cut Peruvian lilies, roses, bearded iris,
display fresh bouquets upon kitchen counter.

At the laptop, I grouse and vent,
memorialize expressions of discontent
within documents I eventually delete.
Time passes. I meditate, recite mantras of hope,
compose a lengthy gratitude list.

A Hundred Songs

Morning coffee whispers,
dribbles mocha java into glass carafe.
Initial rivulets sizzle.

Buffeted oak limbs bounce and groan.
Falling acorns spatter gutter, shingles.
Fog-damp power lines crackle.

Above scarlet salvia mounds,
dueling hummingbirds chirrup.
Foraging blue jays grumble.

A stone in shoe tread scrapes.
Knees pop and grind.
Frozen hips elicit mute curses.

In the distance, ambulance siren, passing motorcycle.
From Naval Postgraduate School floats
the final verse of Star-Spangled Banner.

Sunshine

I dwell in possibility.
—Emily Dickinson

After days of tempest, wind and deluge,
twin rainbows offer a promise.
Hidden tubers unfold paperwhites,
daffodils turned toward earth-warming sunshine.

Daybreak brings a flurry of sparrows,
fluffy squirrels among oak limbs,
untraveled foot paths,
inner and outer worlds to explore.

My frayed soul mends,
stretches its fingers and toes in fresh air,
feeds on pussy willows, pink plum blooms,
golden spatters of poppies.

About the Author

Jennifer Lagier lives a block from the stage where Janis Joplin performed, and Jimi Hendrix torched his guitar at the 1967 Monterey Pop Festival. She has published twenty books, taught with California Poets in the Schools, helps coordinate readings for the Monterey Bay Poetry Consortium and serves as managing editor of the *Monterey Poetry Review*. Her degrees are: Ph.D. in Computing Technology in Education from Nova Southeastern University, M.A. in English from California State University, Stanislaus, M.L.I.S. from the University of California, Berkeley. Newest books: *Meditations on Seascapes and Cypress* (Blue Light Press) and *Camille Chronicles* (FutureCycle Press).

Website:
jlagier.net

Facebook:
www.facebook.com/JenniferLagier

www.ingramcontent.com/pod-product-compliance
Lightning Source LLC
Chambersburg PA
CBHW071012160426
43193CB00012B/2023